D1287213

IT'S GREAT TO BE A FAN IN COLORADO

by Todd Kortemeier

FOCUS READERS

www.focusreaders.com

Focus Readers is distributed by North Star Editions:
sales@northstareditions.com | 888-417-0195

Produced for Focus Readers by Red Line Editorial.

Photographs ©: David Zalubowski/AP Images, cover (top), cover (bottom right), 1 (top), 1 (bottom right), 19, 23; Ric Tapia/AP Images, cover (bottom left), 1 (bottom left); Jack Dempsey/AP Images, 4–5, 45; Marzolino/Shutterstock Images, 7; Red Line Editorial, 9, 35; R Craig Pitman/Shutterstock Images, 11; Bain News Service/Library of Congress, 12–13; Carol M. Highsmith/Carol M. Highsmith Archive/Library of Congress, 15; Ed Andrieski/AP Images, 17; Michael Conroy/AP Images, 21; Derek Regensburger/Cal Sport Media/AP Images, 24–25; Toby Talbot/AP Images, 29; Matt Slocum/AP Images, 31; Kris Wiktor/Shutterstock Images, 32–33; photo-denver/Shutterstock Images, 37; Brennan Linsley/AP Images, 38–39; Michael-John Wolfe/Shutterstock Images, 41; Capture Light/Shutterstock Images, 43

ISBN
978-1-63517-927-9 (hardcover)
978-1-64185-029-2 (paperback)
978-1-64185-231-9 (ebook pdf)
978-1-64185-130-5 (hosted ebook)

Library of Congress Control Number: 2018931993

Printed in the United States of America
Mankato, MN
May, 2018

ABOUT THE AUTHOR

Todd Kortemeier is a sports journalist, children's book author, and massive sports fan from Minnesota. He has authored dozens of sports books for young people and has covered US Olympic sports and the NHL. He and his wife live near Minneapolis with their dog.

TABLE OF CONTENTS

CHAPTER 1

ROCKY MOUNTAIN HIGH

Colorado's sports teams aren't afraid to embrace their unique traits. Whether that means wearing brightly colored uniforms, playing in picturesque stadiums, or adapting to high altitudes, Colorado teams are truly Coloradan.

For thousands of years, the Rocky Mountains have called to people. From the first inhabitants of North America to the people of today, Colorado's famous mountains have been a destination.

Players such as the Broncos' Von Miller have given Colorado fans much to cheer for over the years.

Approximately 13,000 years ago, native people used the Rocky Mountains as a pathway to the rest of North America. Along with the Pacific Coast, the Rockies were one of two main **migration** routes used by American Indians.

Many native **tribes** also settled in the mountains. The area that is now Rocky Mountain National Park was first occupied 11,000 years ago. But native people lived all over Colorado. Tribes such as the Comanche and Arapaho settled on the eastern plains. The Ute settled in the western mountains.

Native people lived alone in Colorado until the 1500s, when Spanish explorers arrived. These explorers noticed the red color of the land and named the place *Colorado*, a word for "red" in Spanish. The first Spanish explorers were looking for gold. They didn't find it right away,

▲ The Comanche tribe became highly skilled with horses in the late 1600s and early 1700s.

but Colorado's land was rich in other natural resources.

In 1848, following the Mexican–American War, the United States gained a huge amount of territory. Part of this land later became western Colorado. In 1858, people found gold near Pikes Peak. News of this discovery set off a **gold rush**.

Settlers, most of them of European descent, flocked to Colorado in hopes of striking it rich. The population in the area exploded. It led to the creation of cities such as Denver and Boulder.

The population boom had some benefits. Because the area now had so many people, the US government created the Colorado Territory in 1861. Some people also got very rich.

However, the gold rush was a disaster for American Indians. Their lands were taken over by **prospectors** who started using up all the resources. White settlers also killed thousands of buffalo and took down trees, disrupting the native people's way of life.

The US government made **treaties** to help protect the American Indians. But the government often failed to meet these agreements. Some native tribes fought back, which led to war.

By 1869, the last of the fighting tribes was defeated. Many who survived ended up moving to reservations in Oklahoma.

The Colorado Territory continued to grow even after the gold rush ended in the mid-1860s. In 1876, Colorado officially became the 38th state in the nation.

COLORADO'S FLAG ◁

Andrew Carlisle Carson designed the Colorado flag in 1911. The flag's colors were chosen to symbolize the state's greatest natural features.

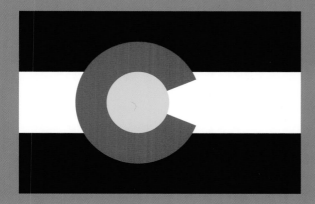

Blue = Sky
White = Snow
Red = Soil
Gold = Sunshine

Colorado's **economy** relied on its natural resources. Gold mining was still a major industry. But Colorado also had coal mines, steel mills, farms, and more. Mining and manufacturing remained big industries in Colorado throughout the early 1900s.

The state's population surpassed one million in 1931. Today, it is more than five times that. Colorado still depends on its natural resources, but the modern economy is much more diverse. Colorado, especially the capital of Denver, is home to many big businesses in the finance and technology industries.

> ## ➤ THINK ABOUT IT

In the 1800s, people left behind everything they had to search for gold in Colorado. Do you think you would have taken that risk? Why or why not?

Interstate 70 leads thousands of people each year from Denver into the Rocky Mountains.

The first people who came to Colorado were just passing through. People still pass through the state. But now, instead of looking for gold, they might be looking for a great ski hill or a scenic mountain hike. Or they might be sports fans. Whether cheering on pro or college teams, Coloradans are passionate about the teams that represent their state. For fans of any sport, Colorado is a great place to take in a game.

CHAPTER 2

DENVER'S TEAMS ARE COLORADO'S TEAMS

With more than 680,000 residents, Denver is Colorado's largest city. And Denver is home to all of the state's major pro sports teams. The Mile High City has more than 150 years of history, but only since 1960 has it truly been a major league sports city.

Minor league baseball was one of Colorado's only sports attractions in the early 1900s. In 1911, the Denver Grizzlies played 165 games.

Minor league baseball was popular in Denver before big-league teams began playing there.

They won 111 of those games and lost only 54. Many baseball historians consider them one of the greatest minor league teams ever.

In 1949, a basketball team called the Nuggets became the state's first major league team. Named for the gold nuggets found during the gold rush, they played in the National Basketball Association (NBA) during the 1949–50 season. However, the team finished with a record of 11–51 and **folded** after one season.

A decade later, another major pro team arrived in Denver. The Denver Broncos joined the upstart American Football League (AFL) in 1960. This league was founded as a rival to the National Football League (NFL). The Broncos won their first game, but they didn't win many others. In fact, the Broncos lost nearly 100 games during their 10 seasons in the AFL.

After some early struggles, the Broncos became one of the most successful and popular teams in the NFL.

The Broncos almost moved to Atlanta in 1965, but a group of local owners stepped in and bought the team. Fans were grateful knowing their hometown team was staying, and they started attending games in greater numbers. Then in 1970, the AFL merged with the NFL. Meanwhile, the Broncos expanded Mile High Stadium to keep up with the increasing demand for tickets.

In 1973, the Broncos finally had their first winning season. They added 14 more winning seasons over the next 20 years.

The Broncos appeared in four Super Bowls in the 1970s and 1980s. However, they all ended in defeat. The team didn't break through until quarterback John Elway led the Broncos to two Super Bowl titles in the 1990s. Another superstar quarterback, Peyton Manning, led the team to another championship in the 2016 season.

The Denver Rockets brought pro basketball back to Denver in 1967. Similar to the Broncos, the Rockets began in an upstart league. The American Basketball Association (ABA) competed with the NBA. By 1974, the Denver team knew it wanted to join the NBA. Unfortunately, the NBA already had a team called the Rockets. Following a fan contest, Denver's team was renamed the

▲ The Nuggets made the NBA playoffs nine years in a row beginning in 1982.

Nuggets. When the ABA folded, the Nuggets joined the NBA in 1976.

The Nuggets regularly made the playoffs in the ABA. That continued in the NBA. During the 1980s, the team became known for its colorful uniforms and the play of forward Alex English.

English was a steady scorer, and the Nuggets teams he led were some of the highest scoring in NBA history. In 1992, the team retired his No. 2 jersey. In addition to English, the Nuggets have had other Hall of Famers such as Dikembe Mutombo and Allen Iverson. However, they were still looking for their first NBA Finals trip in 2018.

Even as major pro basketball and football teams came to Denver, baseball remained minor league there for much longer. But in 1993, the Colorado Rockies finally brought Major League Baseball (MLB) to Denver. The team joined the National League (NL) West division, where it has played ever since. The Rockies made the playoffs in only their third season. In 2007, they made it to their first World Series but lost in four games.

The Rockies are known for their power hitters. First baseman Todd Helton holds many team

First baseman Todd Helton hit 369 home runs for the Rockies from 1997 to 2013.

records, including the records for career hits and home runs. More recent stars include third baseman Nolan Arenado, who won a Gold Glove Award in each of his first five seasons. During that same time, he led the NL in home runs twice.

The Rockies were not the first team to have that name in Colorado. A National Hockey League (NHL) team with the same name played in Denver from 1976 to 1982. However, after six losing seasons they moved to New Jersey and changed their name to the Devils.

Top-level hockey returned to Colorado in 1995. The Quebec Nordiques moved to Denver and were renamed the Avalanche. It didn't take long for them to fit in. The Avs won the Stanley Cup in their very first season. Then they added another championship in 2001. Hall of Famers such as forward Joe Sakic and goalie Patrick Roy played big roles in that success.

Colorado's newest major pro team plays just outside Denver. The Colorado Rapids were an original member of Major League Soccer (MLS) in 1996. They won the MLS Cup in 2010.

Joe Sakic holds Avalanche team records for career goals, assists, and points.

Over the years, Denver has proven itself to be a true major league sports city. With so many people living there, it's no surprise that all of the state's major pro teams play near there. But as any Coloradan knows, the teams belong to the entire state.

CHAUNCEY BILLUPS

Before he was "Mr. Big Shot," Chauncey Billups was known as the "King of Park Hill." Park Hill is the neighborhood in northeast Denver where Billups grew up. Billups was a star basketball player at George Washington High School, where he won two state titles and was a four-time Player of the Year. Washington is also where Billups met his future wife.

Many colleges around the country wanted him. But the point guard chose to stay close to home, attending the University of Colorado in Boulder. With Billups running the floor as point guard in 1997, the Buffaloes made their first national championship tournament in 28 years.

After two seasons at Colorado, Billups went to the NBA. He played 17 seasons in the NBA for seven different teams. In 2004, Billups won his only NBA championship with the Detroit Pistons.

Chauncey Billups averaged 16.9 points and 5.3 assists per game during his five seasons with the Nuggets.

He was named Most Valuable Player of the NBA Finals.

Billups played five seasons with his hometown Nuggets in two different stints. He averaged 16.9 points per game with the Nuggets, the highest of any team he played with. Though he never led the Nuggets to a title, Billups is still admired in Colorado. He was inducted into the Colorado Sports Hall of Fame in 2015. There is a giant **mural** of him at the Buffaloes' home arena.

CHAPTER 3

CAMPUSES AROUND COLORADO

Like most states, Colorado has its share of major college sports programs. State schools feature common sports such as football and basketball, but some sports are more uniquely Colorado.

The University of Colorado (CU) is as old as the state itself. It all began with a single building in Boulder in 1876. Since then, the school has grown into not only a great university but a great athletic department.

The University of Colorado football team is known for starting games with a live buffalo, Ralphie.

The Buffaloes play football at Folsom Field on their scenic campus, where they have won more than 60 percent of their games since 1924. Ralphie, a live buffalo, leads the team onto Folsom Field before games. The greatest Buffaloes football team came in 1990, when they won the school's first national championship.

Colorado State University and the Air Force Academy also have **Division I** football programs. CU and Colorado State have a **rivalry** that dates back to 1893.

The University of Denver, Air Force, and Colorado College sponsor Division I men's hockey. The Denver Pioneers are one of the most successful college hockey programs in the country. They have won eight national championships and produced more than 70 NHL players.

Colorado has access to world-class downhill skiing. And it shows in the state's college skiing programs. In the first 63 skiing national championships, a Colorado school won 41 times. The Buffaloes have sent 35 skiers to the Olympic Winter Games through 2018. Colorado has also hosted the national championships many times.

RIVALRY BY THE NUMBERS ◄

Who has the edge in the Rocky Mountain Showdown between CU and Colorado State football?

First meeting: 1893 (Colorado won 70–6)
Colorado wins: 65
Colorado State wins: 22
Ties: 2
Biggest blowout: 67–0 (Colorado, 1894)
Average Score: Colorado 24.2, Colorado State 12.0
Longest winning streak: Colorado won 12 in a row from 1934–1947

Accurate as of August 2018

The event brings visitors and attention to the state's ski resorts.

CU is also famous for its cross-country running program. Because Boulder is so high in elevation, it is an excellent place for athletes to train. With less oxygen at altitude, the body has to work harder. Then when athletes compete at lower elevations, they don't have to work as hard.

The CU cross-country teams are often among the best in the country. Through 2017, the Buffaloes have won five men's and two women's national championships. From 2000 to 2016, 10 Buffaloes went to the Olympic Games. Jenny Simpson won a bronze medal in the 1,500-meters in 2016. And the same year, Emma Coburn won bronze in the 3,000-meter **steeplechase**.

Colorado's college sports programs bring attention and pride to the state. Not only do

▲ The University of Colorado downhill skiing team is often among the nation's best.

people enjoy watching the athletes compete, but the programs also provide a place for Colorado's youth to reach their dreams.

EMMA COBURN

Emma Coburn's journey to becoming an Olympic medalist began in Colorado—and New Mexico. Coburn grew up in the mountains of Crested Butte, Colorado. When she was 17, she made the trip to New Mexico for a track meet. Emma planned to run the 800-meter race, but since the trip was so long, she wanted to add another event to make it worth her while. That event turned out to be the steeplechase. And nine years later, Coburn won a bronze medal in steeplechase at the 2016 Olympic Games.

Coburn was a star in high school and at CU, where she was a five-time All-American. The steeplechase became her specialty. It involves 3,000 meters (1.9 miles) of running, with the added challenge of barriers and water pits to leap over. It may sound grueling, but Coburn found it fun.

▲ Emma Coburn jumps over a water pit during the 2016 Olympic steeplechase in Rio de Janeiro, Brazil.

Coburn won two college steeplechase championships in 2011 and 2013. In 2011, she won her first national championship. The next year, she made her first Olympic Games. She finished eighth but came back stronger in 2016 to take third. That made Coburn the first American woman to win an Olympic medal in steeplechase. Coburn went on to win her first world championship in 2017.

CHAPTER 4

COLORADANS LIVE OUTDOORS

When Coloradans aren't watching their favorite teams play, they often head outside. And they have their choice of almost any outdoor activity imaginable.

People from all over the world travel to Colorado's Rocky Mountains each winter for skiing and snowboarding. With 27 resorts and more than 300 inches (762 cm) of snowfall each year, Colorado has become a skier's paradise.

Colorado's mountains offer endless miles of hiking trails.

And with high elevation and lower temperatures, Colorado has one of the longest ski seasons in the world.

The world-class resorts in Colorado make ideal training grounds for the best skiers and snowboarders in the world. Olympic skiers Mikaela Shiffrin and Jeremy Bloom were both born in Colorado. Others, such as Lindsey Vonn, moved to Colorado as children to take advantage of the great skiing.

Shiffrin was born in Vail, which has the largest ski area in the state. The Vail resort is 7 miles (11 km) wide and has nearly 200 trails. Other major resorts include Snowmass and Breckenridge.

In 1970, Denver was chosen to host the upcoming 1976 Olympic Winter Games. But in 1972, the city changed course. Officials decided the city didn't have the money to spend on hosting the Games. Denver is still the only city to be named Olympic host and then change its mind.

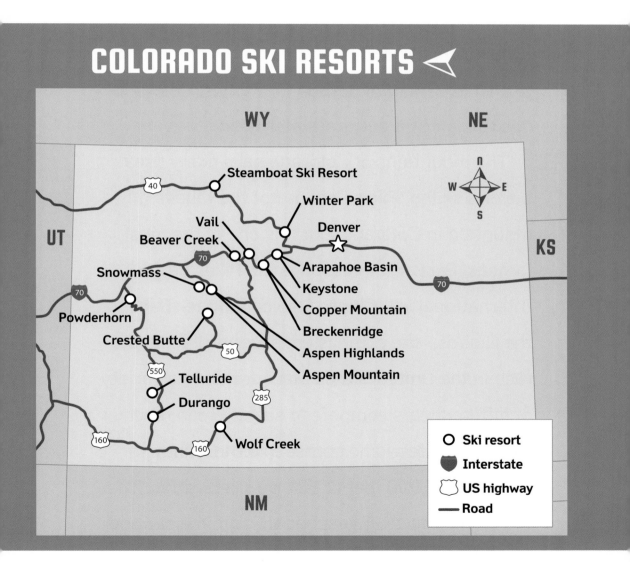

COLORADO SKI RESORTS

WY

NE

UT

KS

40 — Steamboat Ski Resort

Winter Park

Vail

Beaver Creek

Denver

70

Snowmass

Arapahoe Basin

Keystone

70

Copper Mountain

Powderhorn

Breckenridge

Crested Butte

50

Aspen Highlands

550

Aspen Mountain

Telluride

Durango

285

160

Wolf Creek

160

NM

○ Ski resort
🛡 Interstate
⬡ US highway
— Road

Still, Colorado was a natural choice to be the home of the US Olympic Committee. The Olympic Training Center in Colorado Springs provides a home for hundreds of American athletes as they train for the Olympics. Besides providing access to a wide variety of outdoor activities, Colorado has thin air that helps athletes train.

The mountains of Colorado have many uses beyond skiing. Pikes Peak is not the tallest mountain in Colorado, but it is one of the most famous. Part of the reason is the Pikes Peak International Hill Climb. Also called the "Race to the Clouds," the climb is the second-oldest auto race in the United States. Race teams in a variety of different cars compete to see who can reach the peak fastest. The course involves climbing more than 5,000 feet (1,524 m) in elevation. The first winner in 1916 reached the top in just under

⬈ Rodeos connect modern Colorado to its Wild West past.

21 minutes. The record has since dropped to just over eight minutes.

In the 1800s, Colorado was part of the Wild West. That spirit is still alive today with rodeo. Fans come out to see which riders can stay on the back of a bucking bronco or bull long enough to win. Rodeos take place throughout the state. Some are more than 100 years old. The Pro Rodeo Hall of Fame is located in Colorado Springs.

CHAPTER 5

THE WILD WEST

As gold and other precious metals were exhausted from the ground, many towns in Colorado disbanded. Denver could have been one of them, but its citizens persevered to keep the town alive. That pride Denverites had in their city is still alive today.

Denver offers unique challenges among US sports towns. Among them is the weather. The baseball season is mostly in the summer.

Coloradans are known for being outside and active no matter the weather.

But when the Rockies start playing in April, it can look a lot more like winter. The same goes for late-season games in October. The Rockies played one of the coldest games in MLB history in 2013. When the first pitch was thrown, the temperature was 23 degrees Fahrenheit (−5°C). But eventually, temperatures do heat up. Games in July and August have average highs of more than 80 degrees Fahrenheit (27°C).

Denver's weather can also change very quickly. In May 2015, the Rockies hosted the Los Angeles Dodgers. The series included a rainout one day and a snow-covered field the next.

A bigger concern for the Rockies—and especially their opponents—is not the air's temperature. It's how thin the air is. Denver's high altitude means the air is thinner than the air at sea level. And that makes the ball fly farther.

The Rockies' Coors Field is known for giving up lots of home runs.

The Rockies typically score far more runs at home than they do on the road. Even in years when the Rockies aren't playing as well, the team is usually among the league leaders in runs scored. That means the team's home ballpark is a paradise for hitters and fans of home runs. But it's a nightmare for pitchers. Since the Rockies first entered MLB in 1993, they have allowed the most runs of any team.

If visiting teams forget that there's less oxygen at higher altitudes, the Broncos are happy to remind them. A sign above the visitor's locker room reads, "Welcome to the Mile High City. Elevation 5280´." Right before opponents take the field, the sign makes the visitors realize that this isn't an ordinary road game. Winning at such a high altitude takes something special.

But visiting teams keep coming to Colorado. And their fans come along, too. Colorado is a great place to see a game, no matter which team fans are cheering for. Tourists help the state's economy, and they come to Colorado for many reasons. Some might come to ski, while others come to see a game. Either way, visitors to Colorado spent a record $19.7 billion in 2016. And with all the major pro teams in Denver, they can enjoy any sport within a short drive.

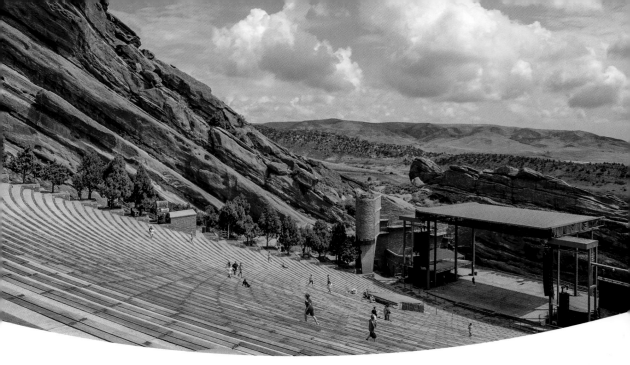

▲ Colorado's Red Rocks Amphitheater is a great place to see a concert or get a workout.

Coloradans are happy to welcome visitors. But don't expect them to take it easy on the visiting team. Colorado fans are loyal to their teams and take sports seriously. When the Rockies first came to town, their home stadium wasn't built yet. That meant the team had to play its first two seasons at the Broncos' stadium. It's a huge park for baseball, but the Rockies filled it anyway.

They set the all-time MLB attendance record. From the Rockies' first season through 2017, the team finished in the top half of MLB attendance in all but three seasons.

The Rockies may be popular, but no team in town can match the dedication of Broncos fans. Since 1970, the Broncos have sold out every single home game they played. At the end of the 2017 season, it was easily the longest streak in the NFL at 395 games. In that time, the Broncos have rewarded their fans' loyalty with three Super Bowl titles. But the teams haven't all been winners. The 2017 Broncos went 5–11 and still

➤ THINK ABOUT IT

Why do you think football games continue in snowy weather but baseball games do not?

△ A fan holds up a poster of legendary Broncos quarterback John Elway.

sold out every game. They sold out every game on the road, too. The Broncos have loyal fans around the country.

The pride Coloradans take in their state shows in how they enjoy sports. Whether it's taking in a game or taking to the slopes, Coloradans get out and enjoy all that their great state has to offer. Colorado is the home of championship fans.

FOCUS ON
COLORADO

Write your answers on a separate piece of paper.

1. Write a summary of what attracted settlers to Colorado, as described in Chapter 1.

2. Which outdoor activity would you most want to try in Colorado? Why?

3. In what year did the Broncos' sellout streak begin?
> **A.** 1970
> **B.** 1993
> **C.** 2017

4. Why does a higher altitude make a baseball travel farther?
> **A.** It doesn't; the Rockies just have good home run hitters.
> **B.** The air is thinner, allowing the ball to move more easily through it.
> **C.** Colorado's warm temperatures make the ball bounce off the bat more.

Answer key on page 48.

GLOSSARY

Division I
The top level of college sports in the United States.

economy
A system of goods, services, money, and jobs.

folded
Closed a business.

gold rush
When people rush to find gold after it has been discovered in an area.

migration
When humans move from one region to another.

mural
A large drawing or painting on a wall.

prospectors
People who search for valuable materials such as gold or oil.

rivalry
An ongoing competition between two players or teams.

steeplechase
A track and field competition involving obstacles.

treaties
Official agreements that are made between two or more countries or groups.

tribes
Groups of people that share a common heritage.

TO LEARN MORE

BOOKS

Hamilton, John. *Colorado: The Centennial State*. Minneapolis: Abdo Publishing, 2017.

Morey, Allan. *The Denver Broncos Story*. Minneapolis: Bellwether Media, 2017.

Whiting, Jim. *Denver Nuggets*. Mankato, MN: The Creative Company, 2018.

NOTE TO EDUCATORS

Visit **www.focusreaders.com** to find lesson plans, activities, links, and other resources related to this title.

INDEX

Answer Key: **1.** Answers will vary; **2.** Answers will vary; **3.** A; **4.** B